In This House Are Many Women and Other Poems

In This

House

Are Many

Women

and other poems

SHEREE FITCH

Cover illustration by Phillip Dvorak, Veer.
Cover and book design by Julie Scriver.
Printed in Canada by AGMV Marquis.
10 9 8 7 6 5 4 3 2 1

Library and Archives Canada Cataloguing in Publication

Fitch, Sheree
In this house are many women, and other poems / Sheree Fitch.

Poems.
ISBN 0-86492-416-X

1. Women — Poetry. I. Title.

PS8561.I86I5 2004   C811'.54   C2004-903573-8

Published with the financial support of the Canada Council for the Arts,
the Government of Canada through the Book Publishing Industry
Development Program, and the New Brunswick Culture and Sports Secretariat.

Goose Lane Editions
469 King Street
Fredericton, New Brunswick
CANADA E3B 1E5
www.gooselane.com

To the memory of my
grandmother
Alberta Doucet Comeau

and

Fred Cogswell (1917-2004)
the mentor and spiritual godfather
of many poets

Contents

In This House Are Many Women

13   The Runner

16   Exit

17   Marie Leads the Way

19   What Rhoda Remembers About the First Five Minutes

20   Filling Out the Form

21   Edna

22   Jane's Observation Notes

23   Charlotte's First Night

25   Barbara

27   Edna Remembers Exactly How It Goes

28   Valerie Listens to Gwendolyn

30   Helen's List

31   The Fashion Show

33   If I Do Say So Myself

35   Neighbour

36   Marie's Lullaby

Propinquity

41   Grand-mère

44   Mother to Infant

45   Villa Madonna

48   In the Still Dark

49   Flannelism

50   Garbage Man

52   Hero

54   Coming of Age

55   This Body Is Growing a Person

57   One Night When Eve Came Knocking

60   Advice

62   Advice from Your Aunt

63   Madonna

65   Cop

67   Civil Servant

71   Grand LaPierre, Newfoundland

74   We Are Sorry for Our Loss

76   Aurora Borealis

79   Miqqusaaq

Ever-Spinning Cupid

85   Puzzle

86   Shopping with a Friend for Her Wedding Dress

87   Overheard Tale

89   When Flesh Suggests

90   Lucy in Parts

90   *The Love Song of Lucy Lament*

92   *Lucy on Married Men*

93   *Lucy on Monogamy*

94   *Lucy on Marriage*

95   *Lucy on Younger Men*

96   *Lucy's Warning*

97   *Lucy and the Window Washer*

98   *Lucy on BUTS*

99   Random Moments

101   Ever-Spinning Cupid

103   Confessions of a Promiscuous Woman

104   Promiscuous Woman #2

Diana's Circus

109   Interior Decorating

111   Monday

113   Tuesday

116   Wednesday

118   Thursday

119   Friday

120   Saturday

121   Sunday

122   Night Shift

123   Postscript

126   To Begin With: Why I left Earth and Other Confessions

128   Cause of Death

129   As for My Method of Transportation: The Slow Toe
        Shuttle of the Clothesline Tightrope Walker

130   First Impression

132   Second Impression

133   When Atmospheric Conditions Permit

134   Woman on the Moon Mission Compatible

137   Acknowledgements

In This
House
Are Many
Women

She runs:

        past men in blue suits with red ties
        men bunched by the elevator door
        men in denim jackets and jeans
        huddled by a cigarette machine

She runs:

        past women with drawstring mouths
        women with wombs puckered out
        from plum to grape to raisin
        women who have never known
        what wetness means

She runs: in this outer space and finds a door

She rests:

        a drummer sidesteps up to her
        whispers in her ear
        I'd like to get to know you
        yesIwouldindeedIwouldIreallywould

She runs: in fear of the lion

She rests
She watches

She appeals to a lady
beneath a red and white canopy
                – what kind of place is this
                and what day

but the lady snaps shut her compact
does an about turn high heel walk away
on her back is a piece of cardboard
cut with pinking shears
words in green felt-tip marker

She reads:
                    I AM APHRODITE

So she runs:
                    past a candy counter of green and gold and red foil
                    through glass doors marked pull
                    past a barbershop
                    through a parking lot
                    to Brunswick Street
                    where she stops before a tree
                    she tries to embrace this tree
                    this tree with bark
                    that is grey and green not brown
                    but the trunk is too thick
                    she cannot reach her arms around
                    and clasp her hands

A voice yells:
                    hey lady why are you hugging that tree for?

So she climbs:
                    (to make it look like she has business there)

but the first branch is too high
she cannot find a toehold
the man who lives on the top branch

spits on her saying:
> *— it's already been sold*
> *this is my tree*
> *go find your own*

She runs
She runs
She runs
She sniffs the sound of a telephone ringing
far in the distance
She follows the sound
She finds the phone
The voice on the other end rasps:
> *— is this the RCMP?*

She runs
> becomes the woman wailing beneath
> the weeping willow tree
> rapunzel rapunzel letting down her long hair

gets up and walks in slow motion sliding image
dissolves to X to X to Exit

when in danger one must
exit to the left:
in one peculiar gesture
a straddling

                              side-step

among
the marigolds

proceed beyond lunar
boundaries
wrapped in

                              moonlight

swaddling

among the nightingales
there is no tomorrow

the secret lies
in perspicacity

in capacity
or rose petal down

                    yodel from that distant peak

in glacial tones

swoop to mirror magic

listen to
bird bones

                    rattling

Take any street in midday heat in any city or town
on an August afternoon
sit down on a bench beneath a maple tree
watch the women and you'll see
high heels and denim jeans
hair pulled back in twisted knots
or freely falling raven locks
young girls with ribbons in their tresses
patent leather shoes and frilly dresses
teens with breasts so firm and full and giggles high
spilling out the secrets they are finding out
women wearing pantyhose and skirts with slits
satin shirts almost like designer ones
in trendy magazines where all the women
are long and lean
listen as they walk staccato on the sidewalk
upright paper cut-out dolls marching
marching marching
then the baggy saggy trundling women
weary of the burdens and the bundles
in their arms
tired of giving
tired of living
but trekking on trucking on
in their eyes all the edges
of the many stories of survival
see this one here is in the midst
of such a story
see how her shoulders hunch
how her step is like she's testing
out the street as if it's made
of quicksand quick get up
follow her

travel past the shopping malls and restaurants
down a narrow residential street
where you pass by windows get a glimpse
of photographs in gilded frames
on wooden tables
see how so many people hang their family pictures
over mantels
follow her until you come to *the house*
one house that looks the same
as all the others but is not
this house is a womb
of many rooms
in this house
are many women

pressing the buzzer
thinking how ugly
the sound of a buzzer

an intercom voice asking: who is there
wanting to say me just me
choking on my name

the sound of my voice
thinking how ugly
the sound of my voice
making
it all too real

doors unlocking
the woman named Valerie
her eyes like pillows
a calico cat on a green paisley couch

a desk piled high with papers
then there were whispers
a kind of chorus:

> someone new is coming
> someone new is coming
> someone new is coming
> do we have enough room
> someone new is coming
> hear how hard she's crying
> she has a little baby

Valerie's voice apologetic:

> can you please fill out this form?

date of birth social

insurance case of

number in emergency

CHiLDREN how many times

Ages are you married

single

date of medicare no divorced common-law?

what kind of how many times of Date

physical?

mental? how many of

verbal? in case where

sexual? how birth are

DEATH ... you

there are rules

how much living

MONEY

been have you ever EMPLOyment

before any current

what is your EDUCATION

told any close

anyone the

of How Long married ...

next of Kin

Phone how long

1|3

Sign

here ✗

I   stop
    cannot   the skipping rope voices
    they   come to me
                    at the damnedest
times like this morning
            I got up while the others were sleeping
started cleaning the kitchen floor
        my mother always said when in trouble
scrub the floor
        that's when they started

        all in together girls
        just fine weather girls

and
this is the way we scrub the floor scrub the floor scrub the
floor
early monday morning
all the way through to
this is the way we go to church go to church go to . . .

garbled voices
                dripping slowly in my head
a 45 being played at a 33 speed
                I remember the days of 45s
remember today
                I turn forty-five
as I look in the mirror
                at my swollen face
wishing I could see
                the wrinkles

Three arrivals
one departure – returned home
see logbook for further details

P.S. we need orange juice for tomorrow morning

Came home depressed. John tried to be interested but he was busy working on his thesis. Jennifer left tonight. Went home. Went back. Again. I am not allowed to give advice. Cannot scream don't go. Cannot say I am afraid he will kill you the next time. Just watch her go. Help her with her bags. Hug her kids. Team meeting tomorrow. I need to tell them I need a vacation.

Can't sleep. Tonight I realized when they first come in they all do the same thing. They cannot hold their heads up straight or look me in the eye. They shred a Kleenex or twist it. But what bothers me most is the way they look at the bare wall behind me as if they are studying an abstract painting. As if they are saying there is meaning in there somewhere isn't there, in that wall, there must be, if only I could tilt my head the right way, maybe I would get it.

everyone is sleeping
the house is breathing
a clock is ticking
it is hot
too hot
the room
smells
like a hospital
Lysol and Mr. Clean
like someone has scrubbed
and rubbed to get
out the germs
the baby is sleeping
in a wooden crib
the bars make a pattern
across her small body
I wear a pink quilted
polyester housecoat
take your pick they
said holding out green
garbage bags
they are old but clean
underneath my window two people
are laughing
that is the strangest thing of all
that out there people are just doing things
like walking and laughing and I am up here
what would they do if they looked up and saw me
standing at a window with bars
who was the woman who washed
and folded this housecoat
and brought it here for me to wear
were her fingernails filed

does she have matching curtains and bedspreads
did she like sex
probably not if she wore a housecoat like this
does she put her hands in the guck
in the kitchen sink at night
when she does the dishes
or does she wear yellow rubber gloves
I know I would hate her if I met her
hate her for having the life
I wanted to have
but tonight I love her
love her for this pink quilted housecoat
for putting it in her green garbage bag
and bringing it here
and who was here before me
and who will wear it after
and what is he doing?

I see him clearly
like me lying in the dark
staring at the wall where
the blinds make a cage of shadows
he is missing me
I know he is
the bed is empty without me there
he knows now he's done it
knows now I am never going back
he is crying I can hear him
crying making that awful sound
the way men cry
the sound of some animal
a wolf maybe
caught in a trap

Barbara

Emily.
she is six
she has a sense of humour
draws pictures of dragons
her eyes are like a rabbit's
pink-rimmed and steady
today I
read her a story
saw a smile
she said she liked
the way the story ended
happy ever after.

Jason. Twelve.
a volcano
today he pounded
a castle his sister
made of playdough
pounded so hard
he made his knuckles
bleed
called me a bitch
when I told him to stop
my name is Barbara
I said
he pounded the table again
kicked his mother
kicking is not allowed
in this house
I told him
his mother slapped him
slapping is not allowed
in this house

I told her
she said who do you think you are
my name is Barbara
I told her
hitting and name-calling
not allowed
house rules
they both looked
relieved.

hey mickey and susie were up in a tree they were
doing the
k-i-s-s-i-n-g-thing
next thing you know
was the wedding bells ringing
and people were singing and ever-y-thing
and waah came the baby
and farmer in the dell
well mickey and susie weren't doing very well
singing ashes ashes
wishes in the well
promises are falling down falling down all
the way to
hell

Little Boy Blue has to pay the bills
Little Miss Muffet's on Valium pills

so mickey said to susie
want to go back to that tree
to the time when we kissed
and the kisses were free

but no king's horses
no king's men
could put those two
back together again

mickey and susie
up in a tree
but when the bough breaks
the cradle falls
down comes everyone
baby and all

Even the many syllables of her name
would indicate she must be the wife
of a man with money
she fingers the gold chains
around her throat
twists her wedding ring
up to her knuckle
as if to let
the white skin underneath
breathe
she has been silent
listening to the others
until:

He has never laid a hand on me
never pushed shoved slapped
I don't have bruises
like the ones you have
mine are invisible
imagine when you look at me
fingermarks like ink stains
underneath my skin
he kept telling me
he wouldn't cheat on me
but he did
again and again and again

I did not leave because of his violence
I left because of mine
I got another phone call
from another woman
I went in and watched him sleeping
saliva like dried chalk

made a rim around his open
mouth
a perfect target

I had a gun
I placed it on his pillow
then I left.

In her suitcase
Gwendolyn has packed
a novel
a flannel nightgown
Oil of Olay
her black silk blouse
because appearance
is important
especially
when you have disappeared

~~Things~~ to do tomorrow:

- get pampers
- phone social services
- tell my mother
- find job
- buy tampax
- peace bond

In the kitchen
a fashion show is going on
Rhoda has a job interview
tomorrow morning
so they haul over
the clothing bank donations
as if they are in the
bargain basement
or Frenchy's
they all take turns
see what fits
what her colours are
dress Rhoda up
then Janet
says let me do your hair
Kathy says I'll do the makeup
Rhoda
Rhoda whose stomach bulges
as if she is five months
pregnant
Rhoda who can work wonders
with ketchup and brown sugar
and Kraft Dinner
Rhoda whose skin is sallow
whose hair has been
tangled since she first came in
Rhoda who draws pictures
with butterflies in them
stands up
    metamorphosis
is a buxom
beauty and for just a minute

you believe her when she says
I used to be a looker
a real looker
but who would want
to look at me now.

There is before and after
and then a before
and an after
again
Rhoda whose voice
is filled with thistles
speaks softly
well sir my qualifications are
fuck all
squeals of laughter
then they do like most other nights
make popcorn smoke cigarettes watch television
gather at the table once again
tell their horror stories
sometimes
holding each other.

farewell
to
welfare

got a job
even got a uniform
how's it look
minimum wage
stickinlickinchicken
the hat's godawful
gotta bobby pin
the dress a bit tight
the stripes are crooked
jeez I look like an
inflatable crooked candy cane

soon I'll have enough
for a down payment
on a mobile home

let me practise
excuse me sir
did you say you wanted
the snack pack party pack
or barrel size
of chicken
that is
have a nice day

then I'll get my
upgrading
maybe take up
guitar again

I used to love
to sing
I've got
a pretty
decent
voice

Neighbour

I will write my Member of Parliament
I will not tolerate this house
in my neighbourhood
it was a nice neighbourhood
before but
last night I saw a shady-looking
character watching
from a car
smoking
drinking beer
I know he was a husband or a boyfriend
of one of those women
I won't have this in my neighbourhood
no I'm afraid I don't have much sympathy
these women bring it on themselves
what's wrong with them
I'd leave the minute any man
raised his hand
where would I go? . . . a friend's I suppose
well, everybody has friends
look maybe it is a good thing
just not in my neighbourhood
I'm going to write
my Member of Parliament

I am the angel of this house
                    house of broken dreams
                    house where dreams begin again
                    house of women

At night when you are sleeping
I sing lullabies
        lullabies for every Edna
                        Kathy
                        Barbara
                        Helen
                        Rhoda
                        Emily
                        Charlotte
                        Jane
                        Gwendolyn
and all the women before you
and all the ones whose names
I do not know yet
who will come after

I sing lullabies for Jason
and all the sons of violence
lullabies for the men who live here
in the nightmares and the dreams
of all the women
hope my song will float and settle
upon their foreheads
like a cool cloth to soothe
the pain fists and words
have caused

I sing lullabies for all the others
living in a house
where there is no shelter

I cradle pain within my wings
sing one more lullaby
pray that someday
in this house of many women
there will not be
any women

Propinquity

Grand-mère

My voice gets lost
in the choke of leaves
coughing down sepia streets

I want to kick the ground
or dig this vacant lot
find a fossil

can you hear me?
                    are you here?

I half expect Christ
to emerge in miniature
on a plastic cross

but there is nothing to be found

only the dandelions growing
from this swollen mound of earth
this whale belly earth
that breathes

whatever happened to Virgin Mary?
Mary, who hung above the kitchen sink
Lady of chipped porcelain
Lady of torn linoleum

Grand-mère

I want your nimble fingers
kneading the knots of your rosary

I need your kiss
on the nape of my neck
your bread dough arms
your brown sugar whisper

jolie poupée   jolie poupée

I think of you often
pregnant nineteen times

twelve babies twelve kids

I still see your shoes
stretched to fit your feet
swollen purple with veins that burst
in childbirth

did Mary, ever, just once
see the skin of your torn burlap knees
watch the scrubbing of back porch steps
plead: have mercy?

did she see the smocking in the camisoles
made from flour sacks
stitched for five daughters

Melvina Lorette Stella Dolores Yvonne

where was Mary the night
a black New Brunswick highway
killed Gary?

Gary my playmate
Gary your youngest son
Gary your miraculous conception
at forty-seven?

this is no vacant lot

                    — you are still here

places left empty have faces
this belly of emptiness so swollen
I ache for a woman
who swallowed the moon

this sunshine in my life this warm growing living breathing
bubblebursting filling swelling within   mine own sweet
beautiful baby   lovethisislove   meaning   the world the
universe is singing lullabies   flesh of my flesh drink drink
breasts aching heart breaking   the rhythm of your baby's
mouth suctioned at my nipple: tug tug rest   tug tug rest
small coos of satisfaction tug tug rest   sweet streams down
chest milk warm yellow slides down sides of feathercheeks:
sleep baby sleep sleep baby sleep sleepbabysleep

There was this woman
in the last pew
in the chapel
at Villa Madonna
that Sunday

It was raining
I couldn't help but think
the drops against the pane
were her tears

grey Sunday
red candle burning
the sisters
brides of Christ
were praying for lost souls
the priest spoke of shadows and valleys
how eyes that looked from windows
could not pass judgement
then:
not worthy so much as to gather up the crumbs
under the table o merciful lord

sisters:
can you pray for me as well
can you take away this ache
can you tell me if my dead child's soul
has made it back to heaven
was it a girl or boy
sisters of charity
shall I name her
find a place in the woods

under a tree
and bury her

it has been so long sisters
sometimes I dream
I wander through a house
hearing the babies crying
but I cannot find them
they are in pain
but I cannot save them
my breasts get heavy and warm
with milk
but still I cannot find them
I wake up and it has rained
on my pillow on my face

I watched her lift the chalice
to her lips
drink the blood
saw arms around her
heard the smothered gurgles
of her womb

all of that
the whispers of the sisters
the rain
the searing sound
of that woman's pain
the crying of babies
in an old deserted house
comes back to me

but so does the moment
when I saw her shoulders slump
in surrender
and knew she would find rest

how many of us
bring flowers
to the graves
of the children
we never buried
how many of us
have split ourselves
in two
as we watch ourselves

live through a moment
or a nightmare
split ourselves
because if we didn't
we would drown
right there
sitting right there
in a chapel
named after the woman
who also had to witness
the death of her child

In the Still Dark

both my children sleep
I know the rhythm
of their breathing
textures of their skin
the way they are curled in dreams

one moans
the other stirs

I know exactly who does what

I am thankful that in darkness
there are things I know

for tomorrow
when sunlight trembles
through that window there
and eyes ask questions
I would rather not answer

I will not even be sure
of my own voice

Flannelism

At five my son presented me
with a picture of a man in a cowboy hat,
bright red shirt and jeans.

"This is God," he said.
"But Mom his shirt is flannel,
that's what's important."

I put the picture on the refrigerator.

I have been a Flannelist ever since.

Garbage Man

on Thursdays we hear the crunch of garbage truck
run to watch the garbage man working
underneath the sun
he is young and tanned and wears no shirt
just cut-off jeans
his hair is honey blond
beneath a red scarf turban
a medallion on a chain
dances on his chest
as he builds up his momentum

orang-utan swinging from truck to curb
half-running half-leaping
with a rhythm that suggests
he is keeping time to music

the sun shining down on his shoulders
sweat-slippery biceps bulging
hamstrings hard as hammers
pirouetting pirate
in an innovative free-style
garbage day ballet

we call the garbage man
Baryshnikov
I tell my children
watch him and remember
when
you do the thing you do with joy
you create a thing of beauty
this is the challenge and the task
of being human:

to take all life's garbage
transform it into dance

I bore them with my metaphor
and my children always wary
of my vision from my window
think he's just a man
in a hurry
to get home for a beer

"We are going to the jungle"
my father and my son inform me

"Be careful of the lions"
I tell them

My son ties a red terrycloth
superman cape around his neck
my father takes a walking stick
dog on leash
the trio
sets off on safari

They are gone many days and nights
or so it seems
for I do worry about the lions
when my cubs have wandered off without me

No need to worry
here they come now

My father is wearing the superman cape
pretending to fly through the neighbourhood
shouting: superman! superman!

My son is running by his side
the dog is yapping
my father in fluorescent red
is making a spectacle of himself

I can see that to my son
this is not a game
of just pretend

My father scoops him up

I watch as they lift into the air
and fly the rest of the way home

My son is in the bathroom shaving
the water runs. I hear the scrape
across his upper lip, the rinse, the tap
three times on the side of the sink
which makes me wonder if this is some
primordial or innate rhythm all men
are born to repeat this razor tapping
male music ritual.

I wonder this of course
so I won't stop to wonder
how it is this child of mine
grew this hair upon his face
it wasn't much a newspaper smudge
of a moustache
but he told me it was time.

It is time
that I am weeping for
how once this child
whose every body part was mine
to clean and tend to
is now a young man
who locks the bathroom door.

Why say: I'm going to have a baby?
You give birth.
But you never own.
You never *have*.

To say baby is to say cherub cheeks and dimpled wrists
warm snuggle bunny baby bundle.
Sure there's a faint echo of crying and smell of baby shit
but both are sweet to ear and nose in conception.

Say instead:
This body is growing a person.
Picture that chalky fish on the ultrasound screen as
infant, toddler, child, adolescent
a grown person with a mortgage
no job, child support to pay.
Picture inside you a temper tantrum
a three-year-old scribbling on the walls
a face full of acne
a lip being stitched
a weeping teenager broken-hearted for the first time
a door-smashing wall-pounding adolescent
a runaway
an addict
a crackpot conservative, a lunatic lefty
a vegan
a vegetable
a prostitute
a convict
a schizophrenic
a tightrope walker, a high-rise window washer
a human trying to be.

Picture yourself inside yourself.
(Now there's a terrifying thought.)

For nine months see baby
an old person with false teeth, pleated face
halitosis, osteoporosis, a bruised heart.

Say:
This body is growing a person.
Be prepared
when baby stands before you
framed in the arch of a doorway
waving goodbye with a promise to call
a baby you can no longer hold
                no longer rock
                no longer kiss and make it better for.

Just watch:
as he goes out
into a world
that most days
is just not   good   enough
for any baby you might dare to call your own.

She said to me: Tea. Red Rose is fine.
I need caffeine. None of that herbal shit.

Now, I am the mother of grief not recognized,
the kind of grief that lies beneath
the skin and itches every second that you breathe.
Pleased to make your acquaintance.

Her breath was sour milk
her owlish eyes unblinking
her voice all thorns and thistles
as it sprouted into space:

No one ever stopped to consider
how it must feel to be a mother
of one dead son and another one, his murderer.

I have no guilt about the apple.
I was hungry so I ate. It was delicious.
But I should have seen the signs of sibling rivalry
that stared me in the face.

I should have known that time
we went swimming in the pond
among the lily pads,
a day when work was put aside and
the laughter of my boys was like
the song of leaves and sky.
They splashed around while
I sat naked in the sun
(my hair takes such a long time to dry).

When Cain held Abel's head beneath the water
(or was it the other way around?)
at first it seemed a joke
but he would not stop until
I yelled: Enough!
I said enough!

There were other signs, more subtle
like the stealing of dessert
the finishing of sentences
the constant competition:
who could carry the heaviest bundle of twigs
home to father,
who could shoot an arrow first and deeper
into the heart of deer or bird?

I had no Dr. Spock
no family therapists.
The only words we knew
were handed down by
God the Father Almighty
who treated Adam and me like
naughty children ourselves.
What role models?
Dysfunctional from the beginning.

Think of me when you start to say,
What have I done, haven't done,
how have I failed the children I have borne?
I was there the whole time every day each second —
except for that once —
and look how mine turned out.

Take comfort unless one of yours is dead
the other one the murderer.

Remember I did have Japheth afterwards,
got a third chance to be a better mother.
Make yours good the first time.
One child who does you proud
does not dissolve sorrow.

Honey, you do the best you can with who you are
and what you have to work with at the time.
The tea's cold. Gotta run.
This is not a dream. Forgive yourself.

You think too much of what you do.

Read everything Gloria Steinem ever wrote
her last book first

Ego is like a hat
useful protection
but it should always be taken off
before entering a room
or sitting at a table
with others

You are not only what you do
or who you love
but you must do to discover
who you are
love to discover
why you are

If you're very lucky
you'll get seven minutes of ecstasy
twenty minutes of happiness
so quest after self-knowledge
and inner peace

Finding your balance
is a lifetime
high wire
journey

Keep asking
who is God

Listen to the chorus within
that sings the way
to what comes next

You can always change your mind

The best answers will always be questions

You can always call your aunt

First: be a skeptical receptacle
of anyone's advice
listen and consider
then use
what's useful to your life

Then: Ditto.
Ditto, kiddo.

And: read Pema Chödrön as well as Gloria
practise the art of waiting
when in a pinch
consult your inner godmother

she's often just as wise as any dear old aunt.

Madonna

real madonnas
are not bullet-breasted singers
making videos and imitating
Marilyn Monroe

they are women who take care
of other women's children
women who
wipe noses
change diapers
make meals
help children learn
to climb the Jungle Gym
while their mothers
climb corporate ladders
in stockings and three-piece suits
argue court cases
or make minimum wage
which pays rent
and daycare

if I could
I would paint a fresco
of a woman with a rope
around her waist
a rag-taggle of children
following along through the park

her nose would be smudged
with finger paint
her jeans splattered
with playdough

in one hand
I would paint
one half of the university diploma
I studied for
in her other hand
would be the hand
of my child

there would be a halo
around her head

if I sold this painting
I would take her to
a Greek island
where someone could take care of her
where there are no children saying
can I could you I want my Mommie

I would call this painting
Shirley in the Park with the Children

Cop

Undercover prostitute,
she walked Toronto streets
where she learned the difference
between psychopathic and pathetic
that vanilla
mixed with brown paper
stirred with rain
was the stench of loneliness
that eyes filled with a film of glue
could spill down upon spit-polished boot tips
that tears could come in the midst of city scum.

She found three children
crouched behind a couch
in fear of drunken fists
in the midst of shards of blinking lights
where the tree had crashed down upon
an almost normal family's Christmas Eve.

Another time, she was the first
arriving at a crime
where a ten-year-old
abducted on her way to school
lay bleeding in a ditch
later, at the hospital
tried to give the mother
some reason why
and this was back home
in the Maritimes.

She does all the usual stuff as well
gives out parking tickets, speeding warnings
locks up the city drunks especially in the winter.

Days off, she works with power saw
clears the brush from land she bought
fishes there for trout
rides her horse
as she dreams about the home
she'll build
so for a while forgets
the world she walks in.

When she was my kid sister
she was told a girl could not be a cop
but my sister never let
a little thing
like "no such thing"
make her stop.

Today she visits
gun on hip
I meet her
pen in hand.

Sisters:
we will the wor(l)d away
in ways that we know how
hold on to hope
as best we can.

Can I help you?
Can I have your SIN?
113-176-630?
thank you.
next
can I have your SIN?
114-456-387?
please have a seat sir
a counsellor will be with you
momentarily

I feel like St. Peter
working front desk
at the UIC office
some have memorized their SINs
others fumble
in zippered compartments
put their glasses on
squint
read their sins slowly
as if they can't quite
make them out
then they sit and stare
at walls or scuffed boot tips
the bulletin board or me
I know the regulars
by name and sometimes
delight them
because I know their sins
by heart

every day I sharpen
HB pencils

my daggers
in case anyone should threaten me
people without jobs
get desperate

sometimes I imagine
the battle with pencils and paper and pen
staple gun

when it is over
the floor is stained
with ink drawn directly
from the veins of sin-filled civilians
and the civil servants
whose job it is
to smile while
we tell lies like

it will only be a little while
then someone will take care of you

there was the time a man
threw his record of employment
across the desk at me
all I really remember
was the dandruff
hailstone-size
on his navy blue sweater

another time I was told
there were no groceries
Christmas was the next week

I tried to console
got spit on

what the fuck do you know
stupid bitch you got a job

one time I was given
a bouquet of geraniums
picked from the flower boxes
in front of city hall
because

you work hard
you make me feel okay
when I come in here

waiting rooms make people tired
tired people live in waiting rooms
that is what I learn in this job
daily I am reminded of regional
despair-ity
hear too many confessions
no power to give absolution
or even a bit of hope that someday
the phone will ring
the job they have been waiting for
is theirs

I quit
the guilt
of my conspiracy
dissolved
almost

some nights still
I wake up
having dreamt
people swivel by my desk
in turnstile fashion
my voice is a recorded message

Can I have your sin?
Can I have your sin?

Grand LaPierre, Newfoundland

(for Ross Elliott)

In the Burin in April
one thinks of the word barren

grey against grey

the hills are stubbled with whiskers
with quills
humped backs
of giant porcupines
outlined against an ice-blue sky

the snow is plastic trying to melt
the colour of scorched marshmallow
the grass is dead
the colour is nicotine

the road to the schoolhouse is long

we round the corner and suddenly
there is a live world
houses like children's building blocks
staggered on a hill
multi-coloured stairsteps
leading to a wharf
the mountains like parentheses
on either side
are hugging all these lives within

the ocean, cobalt blue and on and out
as far as I dare look without weeping

I have arrived I think
to that spot on the edge.

The children and teachers
are awaiting my arrival
the halls are decked with pictures:
    lemon tempera sun and tempera green grass

the laughter of these children
sounds to me like the laughter
of balloons

unspoiled children
ready to ask, and touch and hear.

As we twist our tongues around syllables
I try to explain to them
that poetry is everywhere
the wash of waves
the crackle of fire
that no it doesn't have to rhyme
but it must always have a beat
a finger-snap
a toe-tap
that to write one must see and taste and smell and hear and feel
and more than that, must feel the taste must smell the hear

they seem to understand

at noon when they go home
I walk down to the wharf
needing solitude certainly
but more than that, I have an overwhelming
urge to put my finger in the April ocean
to test the temperature of the sea

as I sit here looking out
I am convinced
that no one
in the world is as lucky
as I am at this moment

I turn to head back up

there they are: the children of the morning
streaming down the hill towards me
small children carrying smaller children
shifting babies in woollen bonnets from hip to hip
holding the mittened hands of toddlers

they reach me, they beseech me to do
a reading for their siblings right there
on that wharf, right there on the edge of the Atlantic
then they tell me stories of their fathers at sea
tell me of storms and new bikes they want to buy
and point out where they live

I leave the village
travel to St. John's
that night I dream in tempera Technicolor
of a poet named pied piper
who was carried off by children
to a village by the sea

We Are Sorry for Our Loss

(for Peter Gzowski)

So now we can't tune in to hear the stutter-stammer of
    your rumpled voice
a voice that erased the static
of downed lines, connections lost,
that voice that hugged us in and hushed the racket and
    the rattle
of ourselves inside our separate shells.
We are sorry for our loss.

Now we have no excuse to linger over coffee with you but must
        get on with all our days
        hang out that laundry, finish up the vacuuming
        make notes for tomorrow's negotiation
        pound more nails
        pick up another fare before our shift is through
        grow the oregano, herd the sheep, pile that Inukshuk
        take off for outer space.

We're sorry for the loss
of all those words that no voice will ever sing the same:
        Pangnirtung Tuktoyaktuk Palatuk Inuvik Iqualuit
        Nunavut.

Before you said them only words
black dots on a piece of paper.
Afterwards, connected dots in a zigzag puzzle
the magnificent enigma of
a people and a place.

Without being there you took us there
We smelled that cod by God
            tasted those worms
            traced the scars of some brave survivor
            heard the song inside the singer's heart
            held our breath as someone told us how she finally
                learned to read
        & golfed in the snow one first of July
        & drank the water from an iceberg in the Arctic ocean
        & saw in the eyes of an elder
        the aurora borealis.

We are sorry for our loss
yet blessed that we can mourn a man who every morning
listened to our many selves and souls

So we'll replay the tapes, the ones tucked inside our heads,
    our hearts.
Rest that voice, dear friend, but not your ears.
Tune in from time to time, for if you please, sir,
we prefer to think that you will always listen as you always
    have
to this maple-leafed polyphony,
our voices travelling through air as yours did
from sea to sea to sea.

Aurora Borealis

(Pond Inlet, 1989)

I started writing
because I loved the taste of words,
loved the song
I heard them singing.
No two words taste alike,
no two words
dance the same song.

Aur-or-a bor-e-a-lis
a rainbow splashed across
a grade three reader
the only words
the absolutely only words
to describe such a shining,
"northern lights" much too pale
for such a phantasmagoric sight.

But there is a better word: *ak-sang-nik.*

In the Arctic at the time of midnight sun
I think I will not
see the aurora borealis.

Leah Nutarak
how must it be
to have danced for a Scottish whaler
for candy?
To have danced
                at one hundred and three in the open air
facing the mountains
        at Pangnirtung?

What must it be like
to live this long
and still move your feet
in a shuffle of joy?

What must it be like to have given birth
and loved
and buried
five children?

Your tears are water pebbles
resting
            sliding
down your cheeks
where time has carved
flesh like the veins
in the mountains.

You reach for my hand
            we talk of faith and God.
Your flesh is velvet
baby powder soft.

A current passes
into my open palm
like some transfusion.
I know this:
you are sage
wise woman.

We have crossed the barriers
of language and generations and culture,

we have found common ground,
a meeting place.

We hug goodbye.
The interpreter tells me
you say you wish
I were your daughter.

I am, Leah.
Oh. I. Am.

I have seen the aurora borealis
in Leah Nutarak's eyes.
This is how I will remember
Arctic skies.

Bernadette can shoot a caribou.
What's more when fresh killed whale's
delivered to her door
she plunges eager hands into guts and blood and blubber
pulls out strings of sinew, rinses each in salted water
stretches them across a board
waits
waits
until sun has baked them
into thread, spun gold
she stitches into sealskin kamiks.

An ulu scrapes the fur from skin of seals
those skins baked by sun as well
cooked hard as plastic
we chew and chew and chew

Hours of chewing
         sewing
             waiting

Bernadette emails, makes audio recordings, gives
power point presentations
notes imbalances of power
writes proposals for funding
read, writes, speaks in Inuktitut and English
has autographed books by Margaret Atwood on her coffee
    table
cooks bannock from the recipe her mother handed down
    before she died
nurses her ailing father with respect and dignity

sometimes determines dates by what the elders say
about this year's caribou migration.

Bernadette loves her children, mothers others' children.
loves her husband, respects her elders, believes in God
searched for her great-grandmother Shoofly's tuli
from Rankin to Manitoba to Scotland to New York
and in between
until she found it.

Some day she'll bring it home to Canada
And place it gently back where it belongs
as if it is a prayer.

Bernadette's Inuit name is Miqqusaaq.

I stumble on these sounds
while my illiterate hands
fumble as I sew
my one miniature kamik.

Miqqusaaq and the elders
name me: Naluaq –
white sealskin hung out to dry
when my kamik's done they clap

(up here
a person cries until tears have stopped
and wailing is permitted)

Miqqusaaq crouches to the tundra
picking low-bush cranberries
then leaps, her arms outstretched

spins around
Look, look, look
This — this — this — is my living room

Miqqusaaq, once my student
teaches me:
>how to live in caribou time
>how to utter new sounds
>how to trust the language of hands
>how to hug the land and sky

Ever-Spinning

Cupid

Puzzle

When I turned to look at you that morning
I discovered your face
       had arranged itself

in   jigsaw pieces

upon   your   p i ll ow

your lips had fallen to the floor

there, I thought, lies Orpheus.

What have I done to you, finally?

        Slowly, with early morning fingers

I tried to

        piece you back together

but I could not find the edges

looked into your ear
got lost in the labyrinth

        all colours blurred

I realized then I must get up and leave you

disassembled   in your box.

Shopping with a Friend for Her Wedding Dress

The saleslady
has a nettle
of straight pins in her mouth
and a tape measure necklace

She smiles a porcupine smile

Precisely, she hems the dress
meticulous
about the distance from the hem
to the tips of the *peau de soie* toes

There are rows
of dresses
swathed in plastic
the soft plastic
my mother warned me never to put over my head
because I could suffocate that way
could die that way

Overheard Tale

Sheila Wellington
is back with her lover again
after a six-week reunion
with her husband and kids

her sister says they:

"just can't
figure out
what's come over her
come over her
walking out like that
in the middle of the night
into the arms of an alcoholic
good-for-nuthin and Harold poor Harold
the sweetest
kindest
hardest-working man
you'd ever want to"

"guess she could only
take so much
goodness
would rather live in some
godforsaken hole
in East Saint John
smoke toke drink and screw
her miserable brains out"

"she'll pay   God knows
she'll pay for this
lust only lasts so long

and who'll be there
to pick up her soul and body"

"not Harold not next time"

Sheila Wellington
is back with her lover again
her husband Harold's got the kids

or so her sister says

When Flesh Suggests

My breast falls out of my flannel nightgown
I look at it
as if it is a creature – living
but removed from me

Why look there is my breast!

when was the last time I was touched
or kissed

the voice of my breast
almost inaudible

I thought I'd learned to live
without caress of breasts

I pull the flannel quickly
back across my flesh
to cover up
the moment
but the flannel brushes soft
against my nipple

my skin is hungry

there is nothing I can do
but write a poem

after dancing
it's the next best thing
to making love

The Love Song of Lucy Lament

Shall I wear mascara?
Should I shave my legs?
Will I allow a man
to fertilize my eggs?

Should I take a briefcase?
Should I take a purse?
Will I be a doctor?
Shall I compose a verse?

Should I go to London?
Might I go to Rome?
Shall I do my fingernails?
Should I buy a home?

Will I find good daycare?
Can I afford the rent?
I just received a welfare cheque
I don't know where it went . . .

Will I have a baby?
Shall I take the pill?
Can I, should I, shall I, may I
Might I, won't I, WILL?

Will I scream in labour?
Will my milk come in?
Will I do things right?
Will I have stretch marks in my skin?

Shall I take up biking?
Should I lose some weight?
Should I take a lover?
Or might I meditate?

Shall I run for office?
Will I cut my hair?
Ought I march to Ottawa
in frilly underwear?

Should I buy some fish for dinner?
Shall we eat by candlelight?
Should I take karate lessons?
Will I be safe outside tonight?

Lucy on Married Men

Married men who want to cheat
Usually have this line
"My wife and I have this agreement . . . "
So you nod, then he takes no time
"So I guess we'll go to your place then . . .
Well, we couldn't go to mine."

Or he might just say
"You're incredible" or
"You really turn me on"
The best response to this
Is to look at him and yawn
Take his hand off your thigh
Soak him with your gin
Look him in the eye
And say
"Why sir, adultery's a sin!"

He'll say he loves his wife and kids
He's in a rut and stuck
Walk away, politely say
Sir, I don't give a
session in marriage counselling.

Lucy on Monogamy

I've concluded that monogamy
Is like some ancient rare disease
Against which most of us
Have developed immunities . . .

At any rate
It's not a natural state
But for me,
Neither is
Celibacy.

Personally,
I'm into sublimation
I read or write
To fulfill my need
For stimulation.

When it gets too difficult
When my blood starts flowing
I scrub out the tub
And listen
To some tunes
By Leonard Cohen.

Lucy on Marriage

I'm addicted to intensity
don't want familiarity
want freedom
want adventure
not cooking up baloney
I need
autonomy
instead of
matrimony

Marriage can be
a good thing
it's just not good
for me
I need my independence
not domesticity

Atleastthatshowlfeelmostofthetimeexceptforlikethismorning
therewasthiscouplestandingintheraintogetherandgettingreadyto
dotheirsaturdaymorningshoppingandtheywerekissingandiwas
wonderingifintensitypermanentlywaspossiblesoallrightsometimes
igetconfusedaboutthisokay

Lucy on Younger Men

I met a young man
At the shopping mall today
He looked at me
In his brown-eyed way
When I turned to go
I heard him say
I want an older woman
Some bad
Someday

He said: You could give me lessons
I said: Yes, I could show you much
He said: I'd really love to learn
I said: I'd show you where to touch
But dear, I do have a confession
I'm not a teacher by profession
Besides an older woman
Wants a man to know
Exactly how fast or slow to go

Yes, an older woman
Wants an older man
Who can
I want a man
Who already can

Well he stood there so dejected
I said: You haven't been rejected
Women have been known to change their minds
Who knows perhaps one day
I will look for you and say
Today, I want a younger man who can
And can and can and can and can!

Lucy's Warning

Beware the tight-lipped
           heavy-lidded man
with zip-locked baggage
he's a vacuum-sealed coffee can

he needs your lips
           your fingertips

and you'll become:

a can opener

to a man
who needs
his mum

Lucy and the Window Washer

A little to the left
no, the right
up a little
down a little
to the left
the left the left
harder slower
higher lower
harder
not that hard
you just missed
the spot

never mind
I'll do it myself

Lucy on BUTS

I'm a feminist BUT I still really like men it's just the patriarchal white male power structure I don't believe in you understand BUT then again maybe I'm not a real feminist with a capital F because I do like lingerie BUT I do believe in equality I mean it's really okay for a man to wear lingerie too if he wants BUT I believe women just don't have the same privileges as men BUT I'm not angry or bitter or lesbian BUT what if I was BUT I'm not BUT I can still be a heterosexual and be a feminist BUT I just don't like labels or group mentality anyhow BUT maybe you could call me an underdogmatist get it like in underneath the dogma of an ideological stance BUT I think just by being here on this planet we're all underdogs anyhow BUT I'm not going to say I'm a human being first a woman second or that androgyny would be ideal because it negates my femininity and really I'm learning to love my body BUT I don't want to be a victim of my biology either BUT I enjoy being a mother BUT I hate the guilt BUT I'm working on guilt BUT then I get guilty about not being guilty BUT I do want to have meaning-ful work besides being a mother BUT right now I have to do the laundry BUT if you want to know more about women's BUTS talk to any of my friends because I've decided no more BUTS . . . but . . .

In the singles bar
The men come and go
With dreams
Of being
A gigolo

In the washroom
Women spritz their hair
And rearrange
Their underwear

In the suburbs
Couples fight
Then make up
Make love all night

In the schoolyard
Children play
And dream of growing up
Someday

In the churches
People pray
That God lives on
And life's okay

In my bedroom
Late at night
I cry sometimes
And hold on tight

In my kitchen
When it's sunny
I mostly think
That life is funny

And when I'm dead
I'll question God
Why all my life
Life seemed so odd

Then I will search
For William Blake
And ask him out
For mocha cake

Cupid
(spinning
red cardboard cut-out silhouette
twirling by a thread from his head
above a chocolate box display
at Shoppers Drug Mart)
is taking aim again

I dart down
the shampoo and conditioner aisle
peek back out

and there he is again
cherub baby innocent
with his evil grin

You'll never get away
You'll never get away

I can yes I can
I can
I'm the gingerbread man

Shoppers look up momentarily from
their study of the shelves: cough drops nasal spray
lotions creams and jellies
condoms diapers toenail clippers vitamins

I escape down the beauty product aisle
stopping to buy some bubble bath
and candles
take the bus back home

Cupid has followed
sits down beside me

I give up
You win

I surrender
once again
knowing
I will always
choose
to be Cupid's willing victim
just because

Whatever poison lingers in my veins
from the arrows of Eros
will not cause my death
as quickly as a sterile life in which
I feign amnesia
forget that love
is the prescription
most of us came here for
in the first place

He smelled like rain on a purple night.
The room was blue. Electric. Our bodies pulsed.
Although I do not remember his name
his eyes were like Paul McCartney's.
For that night all night
I loved him.
Yeah.
Yeah.
Yeah.
In the morning
he was the one who wanted to cuddle.
I noticed then he smelled sour, curdled
and when, blinking once, I turned back to crumpled bed sheets
he was still there
in that blue still room
asking me to go for a café au lait.
I lied
fearing later he would want to hold my hand.

After he left
I saw the room was really the colour of brown eggs
cracked in places.
The mirror was warped
or could that Picasso face be my own?
My liberation complete
I had become all the men I claimed to hate.

Gossip has it
Mona's giving them a hard time
at the Sunnyvale Nursing Home.
It's not that she's ninety-one
arthritic and absent-minded. No.

Seems she gets up midnights
wanders into Romeo Cormier's room
climbs into his bed for a snuggle.

They've caught them four times now
naked jaybirds
old flesh under fresh sheets.

Members of both families
have been notified
and naturally are shocked and appalled.

They feel there is little choice.
Mona will have to be confined to her room
possibly restrained by tying her in bed
or locking her door from the outside.

Newsflash:
Mona, present-minded,
knows Romeo has something to do with love.

     Picture them, faces close, whispering secrets in the dark
     kissing without the inconvenience of teeth
     palms held to each other's breast bones

breathing together in that small cell
cherishing each other's heartbeats
we are here now now now now
ticking away the seconds before
ultimate forgetting.

Diana's

Circus

Interior Decorating

It happened gradually.

First,
Diana papered her walls
in red-and-white-striped canvas
stuck a blue flag
in the chimney

no one seemed to notice
when her house became a tent
when her daily schedule
started to include
lion-taming
sword-swallowing
if they noticed
it didn't matter anyhow

so they would leave
for aerobics class
without her
after a while
stopped inviting her
to Tupperware parties

Diana? She'll be too busy
don't bother to even ask
this week, I think she's
training seals

Diana happily went about
the study of her circus art
pleased that no one knew
the zoning bylaw

no circuses allowed
in a residential area

it was difficult in winter
to keep the big top heated
but Diana, holding a magnifying glass
up to the moon
managed to stay warm

by spring
she had perfected many tricks
sometimes moved the circus
out of doors

After supper, having cleared
the table, she retreats
to the kitchen
pretends to do the dishes

really, she practises her
plate-spinning act
using mop and broom handles
Royal Doulton china plates
from her wedding set

she imagines
each plate
is a person
or a thing
more precious than the cost
of the china

plate one is her husband
plates two and three are her children
plate four is her lover

this way there is an urgency
that makes her pay attention
and improve her timing

wetting her finger she begins with
plate number one
then races across
the kitchen
down the line
until she gets them all going

she hears applause
she is on Ed Sullivan
sighs of admiration
intake of breath
as the plates begin to wobble
slow down
start to crash

she has broken many plates
there are only these four left
but she hasn't missed once
in over a month of Mondays

Diana is the props person
the rock painter
she paints the rocks
on her front lawn
white
yes, just give Diana
a bucket of whitewash
she's delirious
with happiness

she would whitewash the world
if she could
make everything
clean
clean
clean
clean

sparkle polish buff shine
rinse her brush with turpentine
and look:

white and bright and new again

rub-a-dub-dub
three men in my tub

Mr. Clean you old bald-headed gypsy you devil you
Man from Glad
the incredible gift
of your green garbage
bags

Mr. Muscle
how grimy my life would be
without you

dustballs
minuscule molecules
of lint
   fluff
   fur
   hair
would grow to snowball size
attract rats cockroaches ants
leading to an overwhelming question
and death
ultimately death
for all who live here
mop broom vacuum cleaner
assemble
toilet bowl
surrender

hang out the sheets
worn in, worn out
the wash and rinse
of many cycles

froth over
frost over
the cake
which tastes almost as good
as homemade
home-aid

cleaning aids
Band-Aids

to live in a house that looks like the house that looks like the
house that looks like the house that looks like the house

beside it

to look through the world through sheers
from Simpson's Sears
to sit on the sofa sipping tea
to embrace the birch tree
to caress that tree with eyes
that travel up and out
to the farthest branch
to weep about that smallest
twig that touches sky
the world is happening out there
up there
way beyond   above my grasp

On Tuesday, Diana
paints the rocks on her front lawn
part of the job of the props person
is to make sure the entrance to the circus
is clearly marked

In the morning,
Diana trains the dog
to leap through
her daughter's Hula Hoop
rewards him
with a Milk Bone

she plays the radio
on stereo FM
there is a connection
between dog training
and classical music

the dog responds best to:
guitar
cello
harpsichord

after lunch,
Diana takes a scrub bucket
goes into the woods
in search of bears
she wants to teach the bears
to dance
she turns the bucket upside down
sits
waits

there are never any bears
but the raccoons are regulars
Diana lifts them
onto bucket-base

coaches them
in hind-leg waltz

but it is only a minor triumph

Diana would prefer
the honesty of bears
who do not hide behind masks
who let you see their teeth
from the beginning

Thursday

Diana lets herself
be led
to the basement door

lets herself be tied there
the meter man comes in

he is the knife-thrower
he has stabbed her only once
but it wasn't a mistake
he only misses when he wants to

he's that good

Diana admits this is her least favourite trick
in fact she is thinking of cancelling this act
much better to work solo

all the same
she will miss the cigarette they share
after the performance

Friday

Diana has taken a swing
from the children's playset

suspended it
from a tree branch
in the yard

she shinnies up
a rope
climbs
to the tree house
platform

then she begins her act
on the swinging trapeze

she used to perform in a leotard
but this caused
the neighbours some concern

her buttocks show
she doesn't shave
down there

the children should not see so much

so last Friday, Diana
went swinging in the trees naked

no one noticed

soon she will have to start charging admission

o clown diana who juggles the moon and bananas and
cabbages too the eggs in the baskets she spits from her mouth
egg juggler her mouth has so much blowing power clown
Diana who is known to take blue penis-shaped balloons and
twist them squeaking into french poodles and pass them out
to children all clustered like jellybeans in her backyard her
wig is really popcorn and her red nose a tomato she grew
in her garden o diana we won't laugh for you o clown who
tumbles her clothes in the dryer and practises somersaults
and flips

Sunday

On Sunday morning Diana practises tightrope walking
barefoot on her clothesline. The first morning she did this
her washing machine ceased.

     — she sure knows how to hang a good line —

That is what they used to say about Diana before that
morning. Now the children watch from windows. The
shutters flutter like eyelashes. The other mothers pretend not
to notice but silently applaud Diana's sense of balance.

     — it isn't very high and besides, I don't mind a few
          broken bones
       while I'm learning

Sometimes at night
you can hear Diana
with a hammer
in the basement
working by moonlight
she is creating
a merry-go-round
that will run on
dish detergent
make bubbles as it spins
around
and up
a spiral
pointing to the stars
playing a tune
that sounds like flutes
tin whistles
the horses will be unicorns
and wear roses
in their bridles
and when it is done
she will take a megaphone
invite everyone to
come to
Diana's circus

For over a year
Diana held her circus
worked late nights
on the never-ending
merry-go-round
construction
kept the flag flying
she even inserted a ruby
in her navel
learned to ride
on elephants
she passed out tickets

no one ever came

just watched silently
from behind curtains

so Diana decided
to take the ultimate risk
to walk the clothesline tightrope
barefoot
blindfolded

she practised after dark

one morning Diana was found
wrapped around
the line
the way a bedspread
blown by wind
can tangle up inside itself

— she must have lost her balance
— we will miss Diana and her circus

the other women remembered
to only walk the clothesline tightrope
barefoot

when the sun was out
when the wind was just a breeze
when there was no danger
of being
knocked off balance

but Diana's story is not over

truth is, Diana left
stuffed pillows on that clothesline
she ran away from her circus
taking her merry-go-round along
as planned

I helped her escape

she lives where she must
on the moon of course
she keeps meaning to send me a postcard
but happiness makes her forgetful

up there where there are no laws of gravity
Diana free-forms
performs
old tricks

the merry-go-round makes
dish soap bubbles
that float alongside the stars
and the angels

One night walking home in a freezing rain that pricked the skin like shards of asbestos I looked up at the moon. It seemed to me a golden eyebrow arched above the earth. Then, as if I were watching some sort of photosimulation fast-forwarding the phases of the lunar cycle the moon ballooned out before me, a helium-filled cyclopean eye that blinked once then bellowed:

How do you all still have gall enough to call yourself a human planet?

It was not an angry voice more a sandpaper shout that reminded me of dead leaves as they cartwheel down dusty roads, a sound that makes even the bones lonely and the throat close.

A cabbie was driving past & I heard tin whistles and singing like wind chimes.

Hypnotized, I held my face up to the sky until the rain bit my cheekbones & I wondered if miniature daggers of rain on nights like this could stab deeply enough to make me bleed so I held one hand to my cheek clutched my bag of milk and bread in the other tried to run in the wind like running on the spot — picture some human Leaning Tower of Pisa — all the while imagining showing up in the emergency room and screaming:

It seems the rain has slit my face wide open.

Will I need stitches?

& they would tell me there is no way to stitch up wounds inflicted from the heavens

You will need a special thread found only on the moon

Then I would die.

They would write me up like those people struck dead by lightning or spontaneous combustion.

My tombstone would read something like it rained on her parade too soon or rain rain go away only everybody would know the *r* was a *p*, pain pain go away, & still I had not settled on a proper epitaph by the time I reached

my front door which during my absence had transformed into a
mouth to swallow me inside to swim in the saliva squeals of my
children & later
after tucking them in bed
I plotted my exit.
    But why?
    I can still hear you asking can only summarize:
    once the moon has beckoned
    once you have witnessed a miracle of light before your eyes
    once you have been sliced through to bone by a drop of rain
    life on earth
    simply
    will
    not
    do.

Cause of Death

They (those who believed I committed suicide)
decided upon closer DNA examination
of the few skin cells left behind
that overall I was too porous.
I absorbed my own and others' tears
until I was waterlogged.
They call it spongogaglia or simply
Death by Empathy.

Now like Sex in the Pan or Death by Chocolate
it is a dessert that tastes like lemon clouds
those sour devils and sweet divinities
sifted together in an ultimate mockery.

I could care less.
Despite being gobbled up
life remains
juicy.

I savour its stickiness.

As for My Method of Transportation: The Slow Toe Shuttle of the Clothesline Tightrope Walker

The wings I longed for never feathered out from my shoulder
    blades
seeds never sprouted into beanstalks
the cloud I bounced on for a while
eventually gave way beneath my feet   making the sound
of gauze   ripped   into strips

& the fall that time was brutal

I almost resolved never to try again
for fear of death the next time

the clothesline tightrope walk was the answer.

I was brave for one reason only:

I learned there were many ways of dying
endless necessary resurrections

miracles and daily reincarnations

& what's there to lose when there's nothing to win?

Walking on the moon is like wading ankle deep
                 barefoot through a field of baby powder
& the weightlessness that comes with the loss of gravity
               would make any soul giddy.

For over a month all I did was turn somersaults cartwheels
one-hand handstands headstands
bounced shouting:
I am the trampoline champion of the universe
although which universe by that time I could not say

but ecstasy like rage or hatred or love or hurt
does not last (the moon's atmosphere cannot change this)

& so I looked down one night
from my perch on an ancient Ridge of Maria
somewhere near the Sea of Tranquility (which is — no surprise —
as empty as they said it would be)

looked down way way way down
realized that I could see

every   one
               every   where

and if I cupped my ears a certain way
could hear them too.

               I tried not to tilt my head that way too often.

After all, I left in search of peace
                              quiet
                              solitude.

Mission almost accomplished
except when you are sick of home
you do not bargain
on   home   sickness.

Earth.

So small
Round
Perfect (from this height)

It's amazing how many people go to their windows in the
dead of darkest night
hearts splitting wide open like the quartering of an orange as
they whisper their secrets
to the moon hoping
there's a   someone   an   anyone   listening

From this height I see how everyone has a soft spot
tender and spongy as that place in a newborn's skull

Oh. Yes.

Everyone can be crushed so easily —
all that is needed
is the same pressure
it takes   to leave   a thumbprint

on this page.

When Atmospheric Conditions Permit

Siren sounds swirl in crimson whirlpools up here at the
speed of light

Has someone's loved one's heart stopped beating?
Is a child in blue pyjamas shivering in flaming shadows?

I'm warning you scream those sirens in a tandem chant:
        Some will bleed in the name of greed
        Some will die and not know why

Can't you see that we means he & she & child
There's so much love but the world's gone wild

        The babies in the world cry all at once
        (Crying sounds the same in every language)

Hushabye babies hushabye hush
I'm beaming you this lullaby
Hush a bye hush
I can't stop the bombing but
hush   hush shsshshsh

My voice too weak off key
cannot reach down
to cradle you to peaceful dreams.

I pray
by the light of the moon
you find a way to make
a kaleidoscope

that from bits of shattered glass you'll keep creating some
things   beautiful.

For no other reason than missing my children
I returned to earth.

Now I have developed a reliable migratory pattern.

I return to the moon whenever I must
Or when someone I love seems in need of beaming.

Turns out
I was neither the first nor the only woman on the moon.
All of us are lunar lunatics
And there's even a few good men.

William Blake is naked and very funny in person.

Acknowledgements

In This House Are Many Women was first published in 1993. Much of the material in it was written or reworked in 1988 with the support of a Canada Council Arts Grant. I am grateful to Kathy Allison, who retyped the manuscript of that book, and to Mary Danckert, for her gift of the word Propinquity, which she gave to Paula who gave it to me. I am grateful to Susanne Alexander, Laurel Boone and Kathleen Scherf, who coaxed my adult voice in its tentative beginnings; to Jacqueline Reimer whose painting was reproduced on the cover of the first edition of the book; and to Julie Scriver, who designed both the 1993 and the 2004 editions.

Colleen Peterson wrote and performed an arrangement of the original version of "The Love Song of Lucy Lament" in 1989. Poems were choreographed in a dramatic reading at Eastern Front Theatre in 1995. Scott Macmillan composed a choral arrangement of "Lucy on Buts," which the Aeolian Singers premiered at the Scotia Festival of Music in 2000.

Poems from this collection have been broadcast on CBC Radio, CBC TV, and the Women's Television Network. They have appeared in periodicals such as *The Fiddlehead, The New Brunswick Reader, Alpha, Women's Writes,* and *Language Arts*; in many educational books on women's and family issues; and in anthologies such as *The Windhorse Reader,* edited by John Castlebury (Samurai, 1994), *Words Out There: Women Poets in Atlantic Canada,* edited by Jeannette Lynes (Roseway, 1999) and *Remembering Peter Gzowski,* edited by Edna Barker (McClelland & Stewart, 2002).